The
COMPLETE JUICER

The
COMPLETE JUICER

A Healthy Guide to Making Delicious, Nutritious Juice
and Growing Your Own Fruits and Vegetables

Abigail R. Gehring

Skyhorse Publishing

Many thanks to my parents, Donald and Martha Gehring, for the use of their beautiful garden, and for all the years they've fed the family from its bounty.

....

Skyhorse Publishing books may be purchased in bulk at special discounts for sales promotion, corporate gifts, fund-raising, or educational purposes. Special editions can also be created to specifications. For details, contact the Special Sales Department, Skyhorse Publishing, 307 West 36th Street, 11th Floor, New York, NY 10018 or info@skyhorsepublishing.com.

Skyhorse® and Skyhorse Publishing® are registered trademarks of Skyhorse Publishing, Inc.®, a Delaware corporation.

Visit our website at www.skyhorsepublishing.com.

10 9 8 7 6 5 4 3 2 1

Library of Congress Cataloging-in-Publication Data

Gehring, Abigail R.
 The complete juicer : a healthy guide to making delicious, nutritious juice and growing your own fruits and vegetables / Abigail R. Gehring.
   pages cm
 ISBN 978-1-62636-393-9 (alk. paper)
 1. Juicers. 2. Fruit juices. 3. Vegetable juices. 4. Vegetable gardening. I. Title.
 TX840.J84G44 2014
 641.3'4--dc23
                              2013033878

Printed in China

Contents

PART I: ALL ABOUT JUICING

The Benefits of Juicing

If you're buying this book, you're probably already enough of a juicing fan to know that drinking fresh-squeezed juice makes you feel great. But in case you're looking for ways to convince your friends and family to join the juicing revolution, here are some specific reasons:

- **Weight Loss:** Oftentimes we feel hungry not because we need more calories but because our bodies are craving more nutrients. One glass of juice can provide you with several servings of nutrient-rich fruits and vegetables, and it's easier for your body to absorb nutrients from juice than it is from whole produce. When you drink fresh, raw juice, you may find that you don't need to eat nearly as often or as much.

- **Digestive Health:** There's no doubt that digestive problems are on the rise, especially in America. Sometimes it seems like I everyone I know has some sort of digestive disorder, whether it be Crohn's, collitis, ulcers, persistent heartburn, irritable bowl syndrome (IBS), or undiagnosed nausea, bloating, or abdominal pains. While these conditions can be caused by a range of issues, they have the common outcome that when you're suffering with any of them, it's tough to get the nutrition your body needs to be healthy and whole. Juicing gives your digestive system a rest so that it can begin to heal.

The vitamins, minerals, and enzymes packed in the juice are absorbed into your blood stream quickly, without taxing your digestive organs in the same way that the fibers in whole raw produce do.

- **Increased Energy and Mental Clarity:** When your digestive system has less work to do, you have more energy for other things, including thinking. Everyone knows that after eating a heavy meal you're likely to feel like taking a long nap. It takes a lot of energy to digest all that food, leaving little left over for anything else. Not only is a glass of juice less work for your body to process, but the intense concentration of nutrients will leave you feeling revitalized and mentally sharp.

- **Taste:** Okay, not all vegetable juices are created equal when it comes to flavor. You may have had a green juice from a juice stand that made you want to gag. But healthy juices can also be really delicious! Add some lemon and fresh ginger to any green juice to brighten up the flavor, or throw in an apple, pear, or a handful of grapes for more sweetness. Some vegetables, such as beets and carrots, are naturally sweet and are great for getting kids to appreciate vegetable juices.

Choosing a Juicer

There are two main types of automatic juicers (as opposed to manual juicers, which are mainly for hand squeezing citrus fruits): masticating juicers and centrifugal juicers. If you do a quick search online, the first thing you'll notice is that masticating juicers are much more expensive, starting at around $200, whereas you can get a good quality centrifugal juicer for about $100. So what's the difference, other than price?

Centrifugal juicers have an upright design, and function by spinning really fast while the produce is chewed up, causing the juice to spin to the edges of the container and drain into your cup while the pulp is caught in the bowl of the machine. Centrifugal juicers are easy to use, work quickly, and are just fine for most fruits and non-leafy vegetables. You can certainly juice your leafy greens in a centrifugal (I do all the time), but you'll get less juice and more pulp than you would with a masticating juicer. One tip is to wrap your greens around a dense vegetable, such as a carrot—this will help feed the greens through the chute. Also, wheatgrass tends to clog up centrifugal juicers, so if you're a big fan of the grass, you'll want to invest in a masticating juicer or a juicer specifically made for wheatgrass.

Masticating juicers do just what they sound like they should—they chew up your produce by crushing it and squeezing it against the walls of the juicer. They then separate the juice from the pulp, generally leaving you with more juice and less pulp than a centrifugal juicer would. Masticating juicers do a great job juicing leafy greens. On the other hand, you have to chop up large produce into small pieces, since they tend to have smaller chutes, which requires a bit of extra time. There is some concern that a centrifugal juicer heats the produce up enough that some of the enzymes are destroyed, leaving you with less nutritious juice. However, produce has to be heated to 118°F in order to lose its nutrition, which is unlikely to happen, especially if you start with cold produce. But if you're concerned about this, a masticating juicer does spin at a much slower speed and so will create less friction, and, thus, heat your produce less.

In short, here's my juicer advice: if you want a juicer that works quickly and requires minimal prep time and less initial investment, get yourself a centrifugal juicer for around $100–$150. If you plan to juice a lot of sprouts and/or wheatgrass, are willing to take a few more minutes on prep time, and have the money to put down now, get a masticating juicer in the $200–$300 range (you may end up saving money in the long run, as you'll get more juice from your produce). If an upfront investment is of no concern, a masticating juicer in the $500–$600 range will suck even more juice out of your produce and yield highly nutritious juice.

I recommend browsing online and reading various juicer reviews before making a purchase. Not all brands are created equal, but you also don't need to spend a fortune to get a perfectly good juicer.

Choosing Produce

Growing your own produce is the healthiest and most economical way to get your juicing ingredients. See pages 119–179 for more on this topic. But unless you live in a climate that's warm year-round, chances are you won't be growing everything you want to include in your juice all the time. When shopping for produce, think about the following:

1. **Choose organic.** I know it's usually more expensive, and it's true that you can make perfectly tasty juice from non-organic produce, but you're probably juicing largely for the health benefits, and there's no question that organic produce is healthier. Even if you wash your fruits and vegetables thoroughly, they will have absorbed some of the pesticides and herbicides used on the fields they were grown in, and for all kinds of reasons you don't want to put that stuff in your body. Also, produce that is not grown organically will often contain smaller amounts of the vitamins and minerals your body needs. If your budget won't allow all organic produce, at least choose organic for the following, whenever possible: apples, bell peppers, blueberries, celery, cherry tomatoes, collard greens, cucumbers, grapes, hot

peppers, kale, lettuce, zucchini, nectarines, and peaches. These are at the highest risk for pesticide residue.

2. **Choose fresh.** Avoid produce that is wilted, slimy, limp, overly soft, or turning brown. Some fruits and vegetables last longer than others. Dense produce can be bought in greater bulk, since it will last longer: this includes apples, carrots, and sweet potatoes. Of the greens, kale tends to last the longest.

3. **Choose variety.** My grandmother's favorite maxim was "everything in moderation." If you drink a whole head of cabbage every morning, your body's not going to be thrilled with you. Mix and match your fruits and veggies so that you're getting a wide range of nutrients and not overloading your system with any one thing.

What NOT to Juice

There are some things that really aren't worth juicing, either because they're very bitter, they don't contain enough juice to make it worthwhile, or they'll damage your juicer. Many of these fruits and veggies are great for blending, but would be a waste to try to juice. Also only juice fresh produce—again, you can blend frozen or thawed produce, but don't juice. And don't juice any plant part that you're not absolutely sure is edible. There are many types of leaves, stems, or roots that should not be consumed. Here's a list of the most common things you might think you can juice but shouldn't.

Rinds. With the exception of lemon and lime rinds, avoid putting rinds through your juicer.

Avocado

Banana

Carrot greens (not edible!)

Coconut (you can add coconut water to your juices, but don't put the meat through your juicer)

Edamame

Eggplant

Green beans

Mustard greens

Okra

Onions or leeks

Papaya peels

Potatoes (other than sweet potatoes)

Squashes

Wild parsnips (cultivated ones are fine)

A Few Cautions

Juicing isn't rocket science and you shouldn't be intimidated by the process. But there are a few cautions to keep in mind.

- Juicing shouldn't replace eating for long periods of time. Sticking to juice for a few days to detox your body is fine, but juicing removes most of the fiber in your produce, and eventually your body is going to crave that. You can also mix back in some of the pulp to add fiber to your juice.

- Not all juices are low calorie. If you're trying to lose weight, avoid or limit produce with the highest sugar content. These include tangerines, cherries, grapes, pomegranates, mangos, figs, and bananas for the fruits. High-sugar veggies include beets, carrots, corn, parsnips, peas, plantains, and sweet potatoes.

- It's best to drink your juice right away. It loses nutrients as it sits, but it will also go bad after a while, even if covered and refrigerated.

- If you have health issues or are on any medications, it's a good idea to discuss juicing with your doctor. Kale, for example, contains a high concentration of Vitamin K, which promotes blood clotting and can counteract blood thinners. Raw kale can also suppress thyroid function in certain people.

What About All That Pulp?

When you see all that pulp piling up in your juicer, you're going to feel wasteful. Unless you use it for something! Here are some ideas.

- Compost it! See page 125 for composting tips.

- If you have chickens, they'll eat it.

- Mix it into pasta dishes, salads, or into cream cheese or sour cream for a delicious and nutritious dip.

- Add it to soups, stews, and broth.

- Add it to breads, muffins, cookies, or pancakes. It's not that weird, really. Think about zucchini bread—same idea.

- Make crackers! See page 116 for a recipe.

Tips for a Juicing Detox

A short detox can be a great way to jumpstart weight loss, clear your body of toxins, give your digestive system a break, and get you going on a healthier diet. Here are some tips for your juicing detox.

- Plan to detox for 1–3 days. Generally speaking, juice is not meant to replace food for longer than that. Longer detoxes can be helpful in certain situations. If you feel your body needs a 5 or 7-day detox, talk to a doctor and do your own research before you begin.

- For 3 days before your detox, start limiting or cutting out completely certain foods and beverages, such as coffee, tea, soda, sugar, meat, dairy, alcohol, and wheat. Easing off these things gradually make your detox easier and may make it more effective.

- During the detox, plan to consume 32 to 96 ounces of juice a day, making sure your juices are at least 50% from vegetables.

- Drink plenty of water during the detox to clear out your system between juices.

- Drink your juices slowly and plan to have one every two hours. This will help to keep your blood sugar even, which helps prevent dizziness, mood swings, and cravings.

- If you need to make your juice for the whole day all at once, store the juice you're not going to drink immediately in a glass jar with a tight lid, and keep it refrigerated until you drink it.

- Don't plan to be very physically active during your fast. Your body will be processing plenty without the additional strain.

- After the detox, reintroduce food gradually over several days.

Healing Chart

If you have a particular condition, use this chart to customize juices to meet your needs.

Condition	Beneficial Juice Ingredients
Arthritis	Blueberries, Broccoli, Cantaloupe, Carrots, Cherries, Grapes, Grapefruits, Kale, Kiwi, Spinach, Strawberries, Papaya, Pineapple, Tangerines, Oranges, Apricots
Cancer	Apples, Apricots, Beets, Broccoli, Brussels Sprouts, Cabbage, Garlic, Kale, Kiwi, Oranges, Pears, Spinach, Strawberries, Wheatgrass
Diabetes	Asparagus, Blueberries, Broccoli, Celery, Cranberries, Raspberries, Spinach, Tomatoes
Digestive Problems	Apples, Blueberries, Cabbage, Carrots, Celery, Mint, Papaya, Parsley, Pineapple
Exhaustion	Apples, Carrots, Ginger, Grapefruits, Lemons, Mint, Oranges, Tangerines
Overweight	Apples, Arugula, Broccoli, Brussels Sprouts, Cabbage, Cauliflower, Ginger, Kale, Lemon, Radishes, Turnips, Watercress
Skin Problems	Apricots, Beets, Broccoli, Cabbage, Carrots, Cucumbers, Lettuce, Sprouts, Sweet Potatoes

Produce Nutrition Guide

Apples

Apples are full of antioxidants, which boost your immune system and help fight a wide range of diseases. In some studies, apple juice was shown to improve brain function and decrease the risk of Alzheimer's. The phytonutrients in apples also help to regulate your blood sugar. Apple juice has anti-inflammatory and anti-viral properties and helps to detoxify the digestive track.

To juice, cut in halves or quarters and push slowly through the juicer, peels and all. The seeds don't need to be removed as they'll be caught with the pulp.

Beets and Beet Greens

Beet roots (the red part you normally think of when you think of beets) contain calcium, sulfur, iron, potassium, choline, beta-carotene, and Vitamin C. They are also very high in minerals that strengthen the liver and gall bladder and act as the building blocks for blood corpuscles and cells. Just 22 calories of beet greens contain 14% of our daily recommended dose of iron, 127% of Vitamin A, 50% of Vitamin C, and more calcium per calorie than milk. Beets also contain phytochemicals and antioxidants that may help to fight and prevent cancer.

To juice, wash the beet roots well with your hands, removing all dirt, and rinse off the leaves. Juice the roots, stem, and leaves until a stream of brightly colored juice pours out. When using a centrifugal juicer, alternate between beets and carrots to prevent the beet pulp from building up. When using a masticating juicer, alternate between beets and apples to prevent clogs.

Blueberries

Blueberries are a good source of colon-cleansing pectin, Vitamin C, K, manganese, and potassium. Plus, blueberries are a fantastic source of antioxidants and anti-inflammatories. Where most fruits have between three and five different kinds of anthocyanin pigments, blueberries have been found to contain as many as twenty-five or thirty. This abundance makes blueberries one of the best foods for protecting our brains as we age, which also means that blueberries may protect from the onset of Alzheimer's disease.

Juicing blueberries is easy. Just rinse them off and pop them into your juicer. The bouncy little berries have a tendency to try and jump back out again, so make sure to quickly insert your tamper after pouring in the berries. Additionally, try to drink anything made with blueberries within an hour of juicing, as the amount of pectin in blueberries will soon turn any juice made with them into a thick, unappetizing goo.

Broccoli

Broccoli is a fantastic vegetable that has tons of healthy vitamins and minerals. Broccoli is high in Vitamin C, Vitamin A, and also contains iron and calcium. It's also high in protein, Vitamin B1, sulfur, and potassium. Lastly, broccoli is very high in phytochemicals and antioxidants, especially sulforaphane and indoles. Both of these compounds help to cleanse the body of carcinogens and may help to fight cancer.

To juice broccoli, simply wash and cut to fit into the hopper. Alternate with apple to keep everything running smoothly and to reduce strain on your juicer's motor.

Brussels Sprouts

Brussels sprouts may be small, but they're packed with a ton of nutritious vitamins and minerals. One cup of Brussels sprouts contains only 58 calories, but has 162% of your daily recommended dose of Vitamin C and 10% of iron. They are also a great source of manganese, potassium, folate, thiamin, riboflavin, and Vitamins B6, A, and K. They also have an impressive amount of phytochemicals, which help to fight cancer.

Juice Brussels sprouts by rinsing them off and dumping them into the juicer.

Carrots

Carrot juice causes the liver to release bile and excess accumulated cholesterol. It also has an alkalizing effect on the blood, soothing the entire nervous system and toning intestinal walls. Carrots help to prevent kidney stones by acting as a detoxifier for the liver and digestive track. Plus, despite one medium carrot having only 30 calories, it contains 330% of your daily requirement of Vitamin A. Carrots are also rich in organic calcium, Vitamin C, most of the B vitamins, plus iron, potassium phosphorus, and sodium. The Vitamin A in carrots also acts as an antioxidant that binds to free radicals, which are associated with cancer growth.

To juice your carrots, cut off the tops and the tips and stick them in your juicer. To lighten the flavor of carrot juice, add a half or whole lemon when juicing.

Celery

Celery juice is a very good cource of Vitamin C, folic acid, potassium, and Vitamins B1 and B6. It also has a lot of sodium which, combined with the potassium, make for a great post workout drink. It works to replace electrolytes and offsets muscle cramps and fatigue. In addition to all this, celery juice has a good collection of phytochemicals that helps fight cancer, lower blood pressure, improve the vascular system, and decrease the suffering of migraines.

To juice, simply break off, rinse, and juice the whole stalk, leaves and all. If using a centrifugal juicer, juice the celery last because it is very stringy and can clog the side of the basket.

Cherries

Cherries are a good source of Vitamin C. They also contain two powerful phytochemicals, quercetin and anthcyanidins. These can both help to reduce the risk of asthma and lung cancer. Anthcyanidins also reduce inflammation as effectively as aspirin and ibuprofen. Finally, cherries contain a good amount of melatonin, otherwise known as the body's bedtime drug. Melatonin can aid insomnia and may help to alleviate depression.

To juice cherries you must first remove the pits, as time-consuming as that is.

Cucumbers

Cucumber juice is full of Vitamins A, C, and K, as well as phosphorus, pantothenic acid, manganese, magnesium, and potassium. Cucumbers also contain silicon, a mineral that the body uses to improve skin, nails, and hair. Silicon also helps combat insomnia and tuberculosis.

Juice the cucumber with the skin on, as many nutrients are found just under the skin. Cucumbers have a high water content, and so produce a lot of juice.

Ginger

Ginger is a good source of Vitamin C, copper, manganese, and potassium, but it is perhaps most well known for its effectiveness in reducing the symptoms of gastrointestinal disorders. It is also quite popular as a remedy for motion sickness, especially for sea sickness, and, for many people, is more effective in this regard than Dramamine. Ginger also absorbs gastrointestinal toxins, hormones, and stomach acids, making it an effective treatment for the nausea and vomiting associated with pregnancy. Ginger also contains powerful antioxidants called gingerals that inhibit the formation of inflammatory compounds in the body and also have direct anti-inflammatory effects.

To juice ginger, simply wash it and put it in your juicer, skin and all. Always juice ginger first so that the other produce can capture any remaining healing volatile oils still in the machine.

Grapes

Grapes are a great source of Vitamin K, manganese, and potassium. Grapes have become known for cleansing the liver and removing uric acid from the body. Red grape juice, especially from Concord grapes, has flavonoids that can prevent the oxidation of bad cholesterol that leads to buildup of plaque in artery walls. The flavonoids in red grape juice also keep the arteries elastic, which helps to prevent atherosclerosis.

To juice grapes, wash them well and drop them into the juicer. You can juice them stems and all. It can be useful to scrape the skins out of the basket a few times during juicing, as the screen becomes clogged and the yield will be reduced.

Grapefruit

One cup of chopped grapefruit contains 120% of your daily recommended dose of Vitamin C and 53% of Vitamin A. Grapefruit is also a good source of potassium, thiamin, folte, and magnesium. In addition to all of this, grapefruits contain an array of antioxidant-regenerating phytochemicals, including limonene, limonin, nomolin, and naringenin. All of these phytochemicals may help to prevent lung and colon cancer.

To juice, cut the outer yellow peel with a sharp knife, leaving as much of the white pith as possible. After removing the peel, simply stick the flesh of the fruit in your juicer. No need to remove the seeds before juicing.

Kale

Kale is definitely king of the superfoods. It is a rich source of Vitamin K, beta-carotene, Vitamin C, lutein, zeaxanthin, and an excellent source of calcium. Only 50 calories of kale contains 200% of your daily requirement of Vitamin C, 308% of Vitamin A, and 15% of calcium. Kale is also a good source of iron, folate, thiamin, riboflavin, magnesium, phosphorus, potassium, copper, and manganese. All the nutrients make kale an anti-inflammatory food, a cancer fighter, an anti-depressant in some cases, and good for skin and weight loss.

The Vitamin K in kale helps blood to clot, so if you are taking blood thinners, discuss with your doctor before including it in your juices. Kale also contains oxalates, which have been associated with kidney stones and gallstones. Finally, in some people, kale suppresses thyroid function. If you are concerned, speak with your doctor or naturopath. It may be wise to forego kale juice or limit consumption to a couple of times a week.

Kale is a little tough to juice, owing to the toughness of its leaves. To make the process run a little smoother, push the kale through with a wedge of apple or a carrot, a little at a time, throughout the juicing process.

Lemons

Lemons are very high in Vitamin C. Just one cup of lemon juice contains 187% of your daily required dose of Vitamin C and is also a good source of folate and potassium. Lemons are great for detoxifying the body. During juice fasts, lemon juice has a fantastic ability to dissolve mucus and scour toxins from the cellular tissue. Lemons are also a diuretic and contain the phytochemical limonene, which has been shown to be effective in dissolving gallstones and protecting against all kinds of cancers.

When juicing lemons, be sure to leave some of the white inner peel to get the bioflavonoid, limonene. No need to remove the seeds prior to juicing.

Lettuce

Fourteen calories (85 grams) of Romaine lettuce will provide 148% of the daily recommended dose of Vitamin A, 34% of Vitamin C, and 5% of iron. Lettuce is also a good source of Vitamin K, thiamin, folate, potassium, manganese, riboflavin, calcium, Vitamin B6, copper, and magnesium. Romaine lettuce contains cancer fighting carotenoids. Plus the mix of sulfur, chlorine, silicon, and B complex vitamins contribute to healthy skin and defend against lung cancer.

To juice lettuce, simply rinse the leaves and put them in the juicer. Push the leaves through with a carrot.

Mint

Mint soothes stomach indigestion and inflammation and can reduce nausea and motion sickness. It can also help reduce congestion in the nose, throat, bronchi, and lungs. In addition, it's a natural stimulant. Recent research shows that certain enzymes in mint may help prevent and treat cancer.

Oranges

A single cup of orange juice has 207% of your daily recommended dose of Vitamin C. Oranges are also a great source of thiamin, folate, and potassium. Plus they have lots of disease fighting antioxidants that rid the body of free radicals. On top of all this, orange juice boosts your immune system, increases iron absorption, reduces inflammation, lowers hypertension, and increases good cholesterol while lowering bad cholesterol.

To juice oranges, cut the peel off with a sharp knife. Keep as much as possible of the white pith underneath the peel, as it's particularly full of nutrients.

Parsley

Parsley is a humble herb best known for garnishing fancy dishes. But this unassuming sprig is so much more. One cup, containing only 22 calories, has 133% of our daily recommended dose of Vitamin C, 101% of Vitamin A, and 21% of iron. Parsley is also a great source of fiber, Vitamin K, calcium, magnesium, potassium, copper, and magnesium. It's a good source of protein, Vitamin E, thiamin, riboflavin, niacin, Vitamin B6, zinc, phosphorous, and pantothenic acid. Parsley is also one of the best sources of chlorophyll, which acts like iron to oxidize the blood. It's also a great veggie to detox with as it cleanses the kidneys, liver, and urinary tract.

Juicing parsley is as easy as rinsing and popping it into your juicer. To maximize the yield, push the parsley through with an apple or a carrot.

Pears

Pears are a great source of pectin and fiber, not to mention a good source of Vitamins C, B2, and E, plus copper and potassium. Pears are actually higher in pectin, which acts as a diuretic and a mild laxative, than apples. On top of all this, pears may lower your risk of developing asthma and contain hydroxycinnamic acid, which helps to prevent stomach cancer.

To juice pears, just wash them and then put them in the juicer, skin, stems, seeds, and all.

Spinach

Spinach, made famous by Popeye, is high in Vitamins A, C, and E. It is also a good source of choline, calcium, potassium, iron, and folic acid. One cup of juiced spinach has 10 grams of protein and spinach has 14 times the iron per calorie than red meat. Spinach is also one of the highest sources of lutein, which protects your eyes from macular degeneration (a condition that causes blindness in old age), and fights cancer. Spinach also has a lot of glutathione and alpha lipoic acid. Glutathione is an antioxidant that protects DNA from oxidation, detoxifies pollutants and carcinogens, boosts the immune system, aids healthy cellular reproduction, and reduces chronic inflammation. Alpha lipoic acid is both water and fat soluble, meaning that it can defend every kind of cell from oxidative assaults.

Most spinach that you buy comes prewashed and can be juiced as is. If you have loose spinach or are growing your own, just rinse the leaves off well and juice.

Strawberries

Strawberries are very high in Vitamin C; just one cup contains 149% of our daily recommended dose. Strawberries are also a good source of folate, manganese, potassium, sodium, and iron. Plus one-and-a-half cups of strawberries contain 3,500 ORAC units, or Oxygen Radical Absorbance Capacity units. ORACs protect us against oxidative stress. Strawberries also protect against the damage caused by free radicals and contain phenolic acids that may prevent esophageal and colon tumors and encourage cell death in cancer cells.

Juicing strawberries is easy. Just rinse them off and juice them, stems and all.

The Recipes

Mint Magic

Ingredients

3 cups lettuce leaves
1 red apple
½ lemon, outer peel
    removed
⅓ cup mint leaves

Mint helps to relieve nausea and headaches and can relieve congestion. It also fights depression and fatigue. Lemon is also beneficial for digestion and is full of Vitamin C. Lettuce has cancer-fighting properties and nutrients that are important for healthy skin.

For tips on growing and harvesting lettuce and mint, see pages 165 and 167.

Green Zinger

Ingredients

3 cups kale
1 apple
1 inch ginger, peeled
½ lemon, peeled
1 cup red grapes

Kale is a rich source of Vitamin K, beta-carotene, Vitamin C, and many other nutrients. To make the process run a little smoother, push the kale through with a wedge of apple, a little at a time, throughout the juicing process. Ginger is great for digestion and will give you a burst of energy.

For tips on growing and harvesting ginger and kale, see pages 162 and 163.

Morning Sunrise

Ingredients
1 beet

1 orange

1 inch ginger

Beet roots contain calcium, sulfur, iron, potassium, choline, beta-carotene, and Vitamin C, as well as important cancer-fighting antioxidants. Oranges are full of Vitamin C, which will give you extra energy to start your day. Ginger is helpful for digestion.

For tips on growing beets and ginger, see pages 145 and 162.

Gentle Green Detox

Ingredients
3 cups kale
2 apples
1 cucumber
½ lemon

All the ingredients in this juice are helpful for detoxifying your system and for weight loss. Sip the juice slowly in place of breakfast or lunch to give your digestive system a little break. If you are doing a detox for a day or more, alternate this drink with other vegetable-based juices.

For tips on growing and harvesting cucumbers and kale, see pages 159 and 163.

Cucumber Refresher

Ingredients
2 cucumbers
2 apples
1 cup fresh mint leaves

This is a delightful, hydrating juice for hot days. Cucumbers are great for your skin, nails, and hair, and apples are wonderful for just about anything that ails you. Mint calms the digestive system and gives you energy.

For tips on growing and harvesting cucumbers and mint, see pages 159 and 167.

Carrot Ginger Juice

Ingredients
6 medium carrots
1 inch ginger, peeled
1 lemon, peeled

Carrots have an alkalizing effect on the blood and soothe the nervous system and digestive system. They're also rich in Vitamin A, an antioxidant that binds free radicals. Ginger aids digestion.

For tips on growing and harvesting carrots and ginger, see pages 153 and 162.

Carrot Pear Juice

Ingredients
4 medium carrots
1 pear
3 stalks celery

Pears have been shown to lower the risk of developing asthma and to help prevent stomach cancer. Celery helps to restore electrolytes and may even reduce the severity of migraines.

For tips on growing and harvesting carrots and celery, see pages 153 and 155.

Cold Blaster

Ingredients
4 medium carrots
1 inch ginger
1 orange
1 lemon

This juice is great to sip at room temperature when you feel a cold coming on. Carrots and citrus fruits are full of Vitamin C, which strengthens your immune system. The ginger soothes digestion and contains powerful antioxidants.

For tips on growing and harvesting carrots and ginger, see pages 153 and 162.

Skin Clearing Potion

Ingredients
2 carrots
2 cups spinach or kale
1 apple
1 cucumber
1 stalk celery
1 inch ginger

Carrots contain lots of Vitamin A, which helps maintain skin cells. Carrots, dark, leafy greens, and apples contain beta-carotene, which protects against skin damage. Cucumber contains silicon, a mineral the body uses to improve skin, nails, and hair. Ginger helps to soothe digestion, which will in turn improve skin tone.

See the Planting and Harvesting Guide for tips on growing carrots (p. 153), celery (p. 155), cucumbers (p. 159), ginger (p. 162), kale (p. 163), and spinach (p. 171).

Youth Elixir

Ingredients
6 leaves of cabbage
5 carrots
1 inch ginger

Cabbage contains selenium, which helps to slow the aging process. The beta-carotene in carrots and cabbage will lend your skin a youthful glow. And ginger will give you an energy boost!

For tips on growing and harvesting cabbage, carrots, and ginger, see pages 149, 153, and 162.

Energy Blast

Ingredients
3 cucumbers
1 cup sprouts (alfalfa, clover, or broccoli)
1 bunch parsley
1 inch ginger

Sprouts are full of enzymes that aid in digestion, which means your body will have more energy for everything else! They also contain the highest quality proteins, which the body can easily convert into energy. Parsley and ginger both provide an energy boost as well.

For tips on growing and harvesting cucumbers, sprouts, and ginger, see pages 159, 136, and 162.

Skinny Green Lemonade

Ingredients

2 apples
1 cucumber
3 cups kale
2 lemons
½ cup mint (optional)

Apples and lemons have both been shown to help promote weight loss. Kale provides more nutrition per calorie than almost any other vegetable.

For tips on growing and harvesting cucumber, kale, and mint, see pages 159, 163, and 167.

Strawberry Lemonade

Ingredients

6 lemons
2 apples
3 cups strawberries
½ cup mint (optional)
3 cups water

For this recipe, juice all ingredients and then stir in the water until well blended.

Lemons and strawberries are both very high in Vitamin C, providing energy and strengthening the immune system.

For tips on growing and harvesting mint and strawberries, see pages 167 and 173.

Lovely Locks Hair Juice

Ingredients

2 cucumbers

4 carrots

1 tomato

The silica in cucumber combined with the Vitamin A and beta compounds in the carrots and tomato will help your hair grow more quickly and more healthily.

For tips on growing and harvesting carrots, cucumbers, carrots, and tomatoes, see pages 153, 159, and 175.

Hair Miracle Grow

Ingredients

2 cucumbers

1 cup berries, any kind

2 carrots

1 lemon

2 apples

The silica in cucumber encourages hair growth. Berries contain antioxidants that increase circulation in the scalp, stimulating hair growth, and orange vegetables, such as carrots, contain beta-carotene, also helpful for luxurious locks.

For tips on growing and harvesting carrots, cucumbers, and strawberries see pages 153, 159, and 173.

Nerves-Be-Calm

Ingredients

2 apples
8 stalks celery
1 lemon, with peel
1 tangerine or small
  orange, peeled

The calcium in celery helps to calm nerves and reduce blood pressure. The potassium in lemon juice has been shown to reduce stress and depression.

For tips on growing and harvesting celery, see page 155.

Arthritis Blaster

Ingredients

1 orange
1 cup cherries
2 carrots
¼ cantaloupe
4 stalks celery
1 inch ginger
1 tablespoon extra virgin
  olive oil

Juice the first six ingredients and then stir in the olive oil.

The beta carotenoid found in carrots and cantaloupe is a powerful antioxidant that reduces inflammation. A related antioxidant, beta-cryptoxanthin, which is found in oranges, reduces the risk of inflammatory arthritis. Oranges also contain lots of Vitamin C, which is essential for collagen, which is needed for healthy cartilage. Cherries contain Anthocyanins, antioxidants that inhibit production of inflammatory chemicals in the body. Ginger contains phytonutrients that work similarly to some anti-inflammatory medications. Celery contains polyacetylene and luteolin, both of which combat inflammatory arthritis. Olive oil contains oleocanthal, another powerful anti-inflammatory.

For tips on growing and harvesting cantaloupe, carrots, celery, and ginger, see pages 151, 153, 155, and 162.

The Hydrator

Ingredients

3 cups mixed greens

3–4 cucumbers

2 stalks celery

1 lemon

½ cup mint

All of the ingredients in this juice are known to be particularly hydrating. This is a great drink for hot days or for before a hot yoga class. If desired, add crushed ice to the juice.

For tips on growing and harvesting cucumbers, kale, lettuce, and mint, see pages 159, 163, 165, and 167.

Red Velvet

Ingredients
1 beet
3 carrots
4 stalks celery
1 apple

Beets and carrots are both full of Vitamin A, which is important for vision, cell growth, and a healthy immune system. Celery helps restore electrolytes in your body, making it a good choice after a workout or an upset stomach.

For tips on growing and harvesting beets, carrots, and celery, see pages 145, 153, and 155.

Tropical Beet

Ingredients
1 beet
1 cucumber
1 cup pineapple chunks

Beets contain minerals that strengthen the liver and gall bladder, in addition to a number of important vitamins. Pineapples are full of Vitamin C, which strengthens the immune system.

For tips on growing and harvesting beets and cucumbers, see pages 145 and 159.

Sweet Satisfaction

Ingredients

½ sweet potato, peeled

2 apples

3 carrots

3 cups mixed greens

Sweet potatoes are an even richer source of Vitamin A than carrots, making this juice great for skin health. Sweet potato also contains Vitamin E, surprisingly enough. Dark leafy greens also contain Vitamin A, as well as choline and iron.

For growing and harvesting tips for carrots, lettuce, and kale, see pages 153, 163, and 165.

Luscious Lawn Juice

Ingredients

1 cup wheatgrass

1 cup strawberries

3–4 dandelion leaves
   (optional)

Wheatgrass contains high concentrations of antioxidants, has anti-inflammatory properties, is excellent for detoxing, and helps to fight bacterial infections. Strawberries are high in Vitamin C, strengthening the immune system and increasing energy levels. Dandelion leaves help to detoxify the digestive track and are full of antioxidants and Vitamin A.

For tips on growing wheatgrass and strawberries see pages 138 and 173.

Ulcer Healer

Ingredients

3 carrots
4 cabbage leaves
½ cup broccoli
1 clove garlic
3 fresh figs

Cabbage juice is known to help heal ulcers. Broccoli helps to fight the bacteria in stomachs that produces ulcers, and garlic is especially helpful in healing ulcers that stem from alcohol consumption. Figs help prevent constipation, one of the causes of ulcers.

For tips on growing and harvesting broccoli, cabbage, carrots, and garlic see pages 147, 149, 153, and 161.

Purple Punch

Ingredients

1 beet (root and greens)

¼ cabbage head

2 cucumbers

1 cup red or green grapes

1 cup parsley

Beets and cabbage are both cancer warrior veggies. They're also good for skin health, as are cucumbers. Grapes have anti-inflammatory properties, and parsley aids digestion.

For tips on growing beets, cabbage, cucumbers, and parsley, see pages 145, 149, and 159.

Happy Belly

Ingredients

1 pear

1 cup parsley

2 stalks celery

1 cucumber

1 inch ginger

Pears help to cleanse the colon and relieve constipation. Celery, parsley, and ginger all benefit digestion.

For tips on growing and harvesting celery, cucumbers, and ginger see pages 155, 159, and 162.

Virgin Bloody Mary

Ingredients

4 tomatoes

2 cucumbers

3 stalks celery

1 cup parsley and/or basil

1 lemon

Tomatoes contain lycopene, which helps to fight several kinds of cancer. The B3 in tomatoes is also beneficial in lowering cholesterol. Celery, parsley, basil, and lemon are all beneficial for digestion.

For tips on growing and harvesting celery, cucumbers, and tomatoes, see pages 155, 159, and 175.

Metabolism Madness

Ingredients

2 cucumbers

5 stalks celery

1 cup cilantro

1 granny smith apple

1 lemon

1 jalapeno pepper (remove
    seeds for less spice) or
    dash of cayenne

Cucumbers contain sulphur and silicon, trace minerals that help to burn fat, and, similar to celery, the high water content helps to hydrate you, lessening bloating. Lemon boosts metabolism, as do spicy foods such as hot peppers.

For tips on growing and harvesting celery and cucumbers, see pages 155 and 159.

Green Machine

Ingredients

3 cups kale

1 cup grapes

1 pear or apple

½ lemon

½ cup wheatgrass or sprouts

Kale offers more nutrition per calorie than just about any other vegetable. As an anti-inflammatory, cancer fighter, immune booster, and even an anti-depressant, kale is truly a superfood! Grapes are an anti-inflammatory and are full of immune-boosting antioxidants. Lemon juice and wheatgrass or sprouts both provide a burst of nutrition and energy.

For tips on growing and harvesting kale and wheatgrass or sprouts, see pages 163 and 136–138.

Antioxidant Rush

Ingredients
1 cup blueberries
1 cup cherries
2 apples

Blueberries, cherries, and apples are all chock-full of antioxidants. All three are also anti-inflammatories, which can help with a wide range of conditions, including arthritis, chronic pain, heart disease, and even depression.

Pear Delight

Ingredients
2 pears
2 cucumbers
½ lemon
½ cup strawberries or
   raspberries

The pectin in pears is a type of fiber that is not lost when the fruit is juiced, making it good for colonic health. Pears also contain antioxidants that protect against brain aging. Berries are also full of antioxidants.

For tips on growing cucumbers and strawberries, see pages 159 and 173.

Tropical Punch

Ingredients
2 mangoes, peeled
1 cup pineapple
1 cup berries, any kind

Mangoes are a good source of Vitamin C, Vitamin A, and quercetin, which helps to protect against cancer. Pineapple contains lots of Vitamin C and the enzyme bromelain, which reduces inflammation and supports digestive function. Berries are full of antioxidants.

Melon Refresher

Ingredients

¼ medium watermelon, flesh only

½ cantaloupe, flesh only

1 cup mint leaves

Watermelon contains Vitamin A, B1, B6, and C. Its high water content makes it incredibly hydrating and refreshing. Cantaloupe is high in Vitamin A and C and contains Vitamin B1, B6, and potassium. They help reduce anxiety and depression, and help fight intestinal and skin cancer, as well as cataracts. Mint leaves freshen breath and soothe the stomach.

For tips on growing and harvesting cantaloupe, mint, and watermelon, see pages 151, 167, and 179.

Lettuce Lover

Ingredients

3 cups lettuce
1 cucumber
1 apple
1 cup parsley
1 lemon

Romaine lettuce, in particular, contains chlorophyll, which is energizing and builds hemoglobin in the blood. It's also high in Vitamin A. The silicon in both lettuce and cucumbers benefit hair, skin, and nails. Parsley and lemon are both good for digestion.

For tips on growing and harvesting cucumber and lettuce, see pages 159 and 165.

Popeye

Ingredients

2 cups spinach

1 apple

2 stalks celery

½ lemon

1 inch ginger

1 cucumber

Spinach is good for cardiovascular health and strong bones, among other things. Apple juice provides Vitamin C and antioxidants. Celery juice has an alkalizing effect on the body and helps to fight cancer.

For tips on growing and harvesting celery, cucumber, ginger, and spinach, see pages 155, 159, 162, and 171.

Green Grapefruit Delight

Ingredients

1 grapefruit
1 apple
3 cups kale
1 cucumber
1 lime

Grapefruit juice contains lots of Vitamin C, which helps prevent colds and the flu. The bioflavanoids help to halt the spread of breast cancer and to reduce water retention and leg swelling during pregnancy. Grapefruits also contain a fat-burning enzyme and help to alkalize the body and improve digestion. Apples provide Vitamin C and antioxidants, and kale fights inflammation and boosts the immune system, among many other good things.

For tips on growing cucumbers and kale, see pages 159 and 163.

Very Berry

Ingredients
2 cups strawberries

2 cups blueberries

2 cups raspberries or
   blackberries

Blueberries and blackberries contain anthocyanins, antioxidants that protect artery walls from damage caused by free radicals. Blackberries are also beneficial for skin. Strawberries are full of Vitamin C and antioxidants that protect the brain.

For tips on growing and harvesting strawberries, see page 173.

Calcium King

Ingredients

4 carrots

2 oranges

2 apples

1 lemon

Though many dark green vegetables are high in calcium, they are also high in iron, which prevents calcium absorption. Carrots, oranges, and apples contain good amounts of calcium without as much iron. Carrots are also high in Vitamin K, which helps with calcium absorption.

For tips on growing and harvesting carrots, see page 153.

Ginger-Cantaloupe Juice

Ingredients

1 cantaloupe
1 inch ginger

Cantaloupe helps reduce anxiety and depression, and helps fight intestinal and skin cancer, as well as cataracts. Ginger is excellent for digestion.

For tips on growing and harvesting cantaloupe and ginger, see pages 151 and 162.

Sinus Clearer

Ingredients

1 orange
1 lemon
1 cup pineapple
1 inch ginger
Dash cayenne pepper

The Vitamin C in citrus fruits will help to clear your nasal passages. Pineapple contains bromelain, which has anti-inflammatory properties that may reduce sinus swelling. And spicy food such as ginger and cayenne are also great sinus clearers.

For tips on growing and harvesting ginger, see page 162.

Green Dreams

Ingredients
3 cups spinach leaves

2 cucumbers

1 cup grapes

Spinach helps to prevent cancer and is good for cardiovascular health and eye health. Cucumbers are great for skin, nails and hair, and grapes are an excellent anti-inflammatory.

For tips on growing and harvesting cucumbers and spinach, see pages 159 and 171.

Blueberry-Lemonade Ice Pops

Ingredients

6 lemons

2 apples

3 cups blueberries

3 cups water

Juice the lemons, apples, and blueberries, and then mix in the water. If desired, add a little honey or agave to sweeten the juice. Pour into popsicle molds and freeze until solid.

Tropical Orange Ice Pops

Ingredients

2 oranges

2 mangoes, peeled

1 cup pineapple

1 cup berries, any kind

Juice all the ingredients and then pour into popsicles molds. Freeze until solid.

Melon Zinger Popsicles

Ingredients

¼ medium watermelon,
   rind removed

½ cantaloupe

1 cup mint leaves

1 inch ginger

Juice all the ingredients and then pour into popsicles molds. Freeze until solid.

Mango, Corn, and Black Bean Salsa

Ingredients

4 mangos, diced

1 (15-oz) can black beans, drained

1 (15-oz) can corn, drained

¼ cup chopped cilantro

½ cup apple or other fruit pulp

Fruit pulp adds flavor and fiber to homemade salsa. Combine all ingredients and serve with chips, crackers, or fresh veggies.

Veggie Pulp Burgers

Makes 6 burgers

Ingredients

1 (15-ounce) can black
   beans, rinsed

½ cup carrot, tomato,
   beet, or apple pulp

½ cup quinoa, cooked
   according to directions

¼ cup panko, cornflakes,
   or oats

1 clove garlic

½ teaspoon salt

2 teaspoons cumin

1 egg, beaten

Preheat oven to 400°F and line a baking sheet with parchment paper. Pour half the can of black beans into a bowl and mash. Add the other half, along with the remaining ingredients, and mix together.

Form the mixture into 6 patties and place on the baking sheet. Bake for about 10 minutes, flip, and bake another 10 minutes. Serve warm with salsa or your favorite condiments.

Super Fiber Muffins

Makes a dozen muffins

Ingredients

1 egg

¾ cup brown sugar OR maple syrup

½ cup applesauce

¾ cup melted butter or coconut oil

1 ripe banana, mashed

1 cup pulp (apple, carrot, beet, and/or ginger is best)

1 cup whole wheat OR brown rice flour

½ cup rolled oats

1 teaspoon cinnamon

1 teaspoon baking soda

1 teaspoon baking powder

Preheat oven to 375°F and grease a 12-cup muffin tin. Beat together the egg, brown sugar or maple syrup, applesauce, and butter or coconut oil. Add the banana and pulp and mash together.

In a separate bowl, whisk together all the dry ingredients. Add to the wet ingredients and stir just to combine.

Divide batter between muffin cups and bake about 20 minutes or until tops are golden and springy to the touch.

Juice Pulp Sorbet

Ingredients
3 cups fruit pulp

4 ripe bananas

Dash cinnamon, ginger, or
nutmeg (optional)

Freeze the pulp in ice cube trays and then pulse in a blender or food processor, along with the bananas and spices. Scoop into bowls and serve. Leftovers can be frozen again in ice cube trays and then re-blended to serve.

Pulp Crackers

Ingredients

2 cups vegetable pulp

½ cup flax meal or chia seeds (or a mixture)

1 tablespoon tamari

½ cup water

Cayenne, or other spices to taste

Combine all ingredients in a food processor. Spread on a food dehydrator sheet or on a well-greased baking pan. Score into squares. Dehydrate or bake at 120°F for about 12 hours, flip, and dehydrate for another 12 hours.

Veggie Dip

Ingredients

1 cup vegetable pulp

2 cups plain yogurt

1 teaspoon fresh cilantro, finely chopped

1 teaspoon lemon juice

½ teaspoon salt

1 clove garlic, minced (optional)

Mix all ingredients together and serve with crackers, chips, or vegetable sticks.

Fruit Dip

Ingredients

1 cup fruit pulp

2 cups vanilla yogurt

Handful of sliced almonds

Combine the fruit pulp and yogurt. Sprinkle with sliced almonds and serve with sliced fresh fruit or berries.

PART II:
GARDENING GUIDE

The Benefits of Growing Your Own

If you've never picked fruits and vegetables directly from an organic garden, tossed them in your juicer, and taken that first, delightful sip, you're in for a shock of the best possible kind. There's nothing quite like that incredibly fresh flavor and the way your body feels soaking up all those nutrients. The longer a fruit or vegetable is detached from its plant, the more nutrients it loses. Studies have shown that vegetables on supermarket shelves may have lost up to 45% of their nutritional value. That means you'd have to eat or drink almost twice as much to get the same nutritional benefits! It's no wonder so many people feel unsatisfied after a properly portioned "healthy" meal and wind up eating way more than they need to in terms of calorie consumption and still don't get what they need in terms of nutrition.

When you grow your own food, you also can be sure your food is free from unhealthy pesticides and herbicides, and is not genetically modified. You'll have greater peace of mind knowing your food is safe, and you'll have the satisfaction of providing real nutrition for yourself, your family, and your friends.

Finally, growing your own produce saves money. It takes a lot of fruits and vegetables to make juice. Yes, you end up with a powerhouse glass of nutrition and flavor, but if you're buying all that organic produce from the grocery store or even the farmer's market, that's going to be a really expensive glass of juice. A pack of 500 organic lettuce seeds might cost you $3.50. Just think about how much 500 heads of organic lettuce would cost you at your local grocery store! Yes, gardening takes time, and time is money, but if you're able to fit a garden into your space and your schedule, you'll be saving some serious bucks.

How to Start Your Own Outdoor Organic Garden

1)   Choose a Site for Your Garden

Think small, at least at first. A small garden takes less work and materials than a large one. If done well, a 4 x 4-ft. garden will yield enough vegetables and fruit for you and your family to enjoy. Find a spot that receives at least 6 hours of sunlight a day.

2)   Make a Plan

Sketch out how you will arrange your plants. Some plants aid each other's growth when planted in proximity; others inhibit each other. Refer to the companion planting charts below and on the following pages.

Vegetables

Type	Companion plant(s)	Avoid
Asparagus	Tomatoes, parsley, basil	Onion, garlic, potatoes
Beans	Eggplant	Tomatoes, onion, kales
Beets	Mint	Runner beans
Broccoli	Onion, garlic, leeks	Tomatoes, peppers, mustard
Cabbage	Onion, garlic, leeks	Tomatoes, peppers, beans
Carrot	Leeks, beans	Radish

Continued on next page

Continued from previous page

Type	Companion plant(s)	Avoid
Celery	Daisies, snapdragons	Corn, aster flower
Corn	Legumes, squash, cucumber	Tomatoes, celery
Cucumber	Radishes, beets, carrots	Tomatoes
Eggplant	Marigolds, mint	Runner beans
Leeks	Carrots	Legumes
Lettuce	Radish, carrots	Celery, cabbage, parsley
Melon	Pumpkin, squash	None
Peppers	Tomatoes	Beans, cabbage, kale
Onion	Carrots	Peas, beans
Peas	Beans, corn	Onion, garlic
Potato	Horseradish	Tomatoes, cucumber
Tomatoes	Carrots, celery, parsley	Corn, peas, potato, kale

Herbs

Type	Companion Plant(s)	Avoid
Basil	Chamomile, anise	Sage
Chamomile	Basil, cabbage	Other herbs (it will become oily)
Cilantro	Beans, peas	None
Chives	Carrots	Peas, beans

Type	Companion plant(s)	Avoid
Dill	Cabbage, cucumber	Tomatoes, carrots
Fennel	Dill	Everything else
Garlic	Cucumber, peas, lettuce	None
Oregano	Basil, peppers	None
Peppermint	Broccoli, cabbage	None
Rosemary	Sage, beans, carrots	None
Sage	Rosemary, beans	None
Summer savory	Onion, green beans	None

3) Make a Compost Pile

Compost is the main ingredient for creating and maintaining rich, fertile soil. You can use most organic materials to make compost that will provide your soil with essential nutrients. Choose a level, well-drained site, preferably near your garden. You can purchase a composting bin, make your own out of wood or chicken wire, or build a pile directly on the ground (if you're in an urban or suburban area, check regulations to see if a rodent-proof bin is required). The pile should be about 3 feet or more in circumference, and no more than 5 feet tall. The pile should stay moist, and needs to be turned every once in a while to make sure there's enough oxygen throughout the pile. You can turn the pile simply by using a shovel to mix it up every day or two. Grass clippings, leaves, eggshells, and fruit and vegetable scraps are all excellent composting materials.

Good Composting Materials:

Coffee grounds

Corn cobs

Corn stalks

Food scraps

Grass clippings

Hedge trimmings

Livestock manure

Plant stalks

Pine needles

Old potting soil

Sawdust

Seaweed

Straw

Tea bags

Tree leaves and twigs

Vegetable scraps

Weeds without seed heads

Wood chips

Woody brush

Avoid Using:

Bread and grains

Cooking oil

Dairy products

Dead animals

Diseased plant material

Dog or cat manure

Grease or oily foods

Meat or fish scraps

Noxious or invasive weeds

Weeds with seed heads

4) Add Soil

In order to have a thriving organic garden, you must have excellent soil. Adding organic material (such as that in your compost pile) to your existing soil will only make it better. Soil containing copious amounts of organic material is very good for your garden. Organically rich soil:

- Nourishes your plants without any chemicals,keeping them natural

- Is easy to use when planting seeds or seedlings, and it also allows for weeds to be more easily picked

- Is softer than chemically treated soil, so the roots of your plants can spread and grow deeper

- Helps water and air find the roots

5) Plant and Water

Refer to the instructions on pages 141–179 to learn how to plant various vegetables and fruits. If you live in a cooler region with a shorter growing period, you will want to start some of your plants indoors. To do this, obtain plug flats (trays separated into many small cups or "cells") or make your own small planters by poking holes in the bottom of paper cups. Fill the cups two-thirds full with potting soil or composted soil. Bury the seed at the recommended depth, according to the instructions on the package. Tamp down the soil lightly and water. Keep the seedlings in a warm, well-lit place, such as the kitchen, to encourage germination. Once the weather begins to warm up and you are fairly certain you won't be getting any more frosts (you can contact your local extension office to find out the last "frost free" date for your area) you can begin to acclimate your seedlings to the great outdoors. First place them in a partially shady spot outdoors that is protected from strong wind. After a couple of days, move them into direct sunlight, and then finally transplant them to the garden.

Water your plants at the appropriate time of day. Early morning or night is the best time for watering, as evaporation is less likely to occur at these times. Do not water your plants when it is extremely windy outside. Wind will prevent the water from reaching the soil where you want it to go. Adding mulch around your plants can help to keep moisture in.

6)   Weed Control

Weeds are invasive to your garden plants and thus must be removed in order for your organic garden to grow efficiently. Common weeds that can invade your garden are ivy, mint, and dandelions. Using a sharp hoe, go over each area of exposed soil frequently to keep weeds from sprouting. Also, plucking off the green portions of weeds will deprive them of the nutrients they need to survive. Gently pull out weeds by hand to remove their root systems and to stop continued growth. Be careful when weeding around established plants so you don't uproot them as well. Mulch unplanted areas of your garden so that weeds will be less likely to grow. You can find organic mulches, such as wood chips and grass clippings, at your local garden store.

These mulches will not only discourage weed growth but will also eventually break down and help enrich the soil. Mulching also helps regulate soil temperatures and helps in conserving water by decreasing evaporation.

Growing in Containers

Container gardening is one of the most efficient methods for growing vegetables in a limited space. Almost any vegetable can be grown in a container—even pumpkins—although plants that take up a great deal of space are not practical. Miniature varieties of vegetables are especially suited to container growing: they require less space than full-sized varieties and mature earlier. Many vegetables can be container-raised indoors as well as outdoors. Leaf crops can be grown indoors even in winter with the aid of fluorescent lights. Fruit crops, such as tomatoes, can be grown indoors but need warm temperatures and at least six hours of summer sunlight.

Almost any sturdy, water-resistant receptacle can be used for container gardening: plastic or galvanized iron garbage cans, redwood planters, 2-gallon or 5-gallon buckets, even a plastic garbage bag. Of course, any type of container must be provided with holes for drainage. Recommended practice is to drill drainage holes just above the bottom rather than in it. Purchase organic potting soil to give your plants the best chance of thriving. You can make your own potting soil mix (you'll find lots of recipes online), but it takes a number of ingredients to make a soil that is light, drains well, and has the nutrients your plants need. Good potting soil is usually a mixture of compost, manure, sphagnum peat moss or coconut coir, and fertilizers.

Because of the intensive care they get, container-grown plants can be spaced much closer together than if they were planted in an ordinary garden. The chart below gives recommended space and soil allowances for a number of popular vegetables. Plants grown in containers need watering more frequently than they would in a garden—as often as once a day in hot, dry weather. To check for moisture, probe the top 2 in. of soil with your finger. If the soil is dry, soak it thoroughly until water runs out at the bottom of the container. You should also add fertilizer every three weeks. Use light doses, however; over-fertilizing can damage or kill plants that are grown in containers.

What to Plant Where

For the windowsill:

Carrots, Cress, Lettuce, Mustard, Radishes, Spinach, Tomatoes, Zucchini

For balcony, rooftop, or window box:

Any windowsill vegetables plus: Beans, Broccoli, Brussels, Cabbage, Cucumbers, Peppers, Sprouts, Squash, Tomatoes, Turnips

Indoors under lights:

Beets, Carrots, Cucumbers, Celery, Chinese Cabbage, Endive, Onions, Radishes, Watercress

Vegetable	Minimum container size	Number of plants per container
Beets	1 pt.	2–3 plants; in larger containers space 2" apart
Broccoli	5 gal.	1 plant
Cabbage	5 gal.	1 plant; in larger containers space 12" apart
Carrots	1 pt.	3–4 plants; in larger containers space 1"–2" apart
Cucumbers	5 gal.	2 plants. Train vertically.
Kale	5 gal.	3–4 plants; in larger containers space 16" apart
Lettuce	½ gal.	1 plant; in larger containers space 10" apart
Peppers	2 gal.	1 plant
Radishes	1 pt.	4–5 plants per pot; in larger containers space 1" apart
Spinach	1 pt.	1 plant per pot; in larger containers space 5" apart
Summer squash and zucchini	5 gal.	1 plant
Tomatoes (dwarf)	5 gal.	1 plant
Tomatoes (standard)	1 ½ qt.	1 plant

Growing on Windowsills, Balconies, or Rooftops

Apartment dwellers can use windowsills, balconies, and rooftops to raise surprisingly large crops of homegrown vegetables. According to one expert, as many as 100 carrots, 50 beets, and 50 cherry tomatoes can be harvested from a dozen 8-in. pots. The most practical vegetables for the windowsill farmer are those that need little space and give high yields. The nature of your space also determines what you can grow. If you have balcony or rooftop space, climbers—such as standard tomatoes and cucumbers—are practical. For a windowsill concentrate on such low-growing vegetables as lettuce, spinach, carrots, and dwarf tomatoes. Daylight exposure is also important, since indoor plants have the same needs for light and warmth as those grown outdoors. For an east-facing window the choice is limited to leafy vegetables and radishes. Southern and western windows are suitable for most vegetables. Warmth lovers, such as tomatoes and beans, do best in a southern exposure. A northern window is unsuitable for vegetables unless artificial lighting is provided as a supplement.

Gardening Under Lights

Vegetables need ample light to flourish, especially rays from the blue and red ends of the spectrum. Normally these rays are supplied by the sun, but fluorescent tubes can take the place of natural sunlight. An equal number of cool-white (rich in blue) and warm-white or natural tubes (rich in red) seem to give the best result. Tubes especially designed for indoor gardening, high in both blue and red wavelengths, are also available. Some growers use incandescent lamps to augment the red end of the spectrum, but these consume much more electricity for the light produced. In addition, they must be used with caution because of the heat they generate. Fluorescent tubes should be positioned 6 to 12 in. above the plants: light intensity diminishes rapidly as distance increases. A fixture with four 4-ft. tubes provides enough light for a 3- by 4-ft. area. Vegetables require 13 to 18 hours of artificial light per day. They also need a resting period of darkness. Leafy and root vegetables are easiest to grow under lights; tomatoes require extra care.

Microgreens, Sprouts, and Wheatgrass

If you have limited space and want maximum nutrition, start by planting microgreens, sprouts, and/or wheatgrass. These are easy to grow indoors and are packed with nutrients.

Microgreens

Microgreens are leafy greens and herbs that are harvested while they're still very young. They have a milder flavor than full-grown greens, which might be appealing if you're new to juicing and not accustomed to the stronger flavors of some greens. Microgreens include arugula, basil, beets, kale, and cilantro. You'll need a lot of little greens to make enough juice to count, so if space allows, choose containers that are about a foot long and 3 in. deep (see notes above for choosing a good container). Add potting soil to the container, leaving about an inch of space at the top. Space the microgreen seeds about ⅛ in. apart and cover with a thin layer of soil. Water lightly and place in a windowsill or other sunny spot. It may help to cover the pot with a moist paper towel to help keep the moisture in. Sprinkle the paper towel with water every day until you see sprouts appearing on your plants, and then remove the paper towel. Once the sprouts appear, mist the plants daily—the leaves will be delicate, so you don't want to douse them with water. In about 2 weeks, the leaves should be 1–2 in. long and you can pick and juice them! You may wish to plant a few containers of microgreens a few days apart so that you have a rotating supply of greens.

Sprouts

Seed sprouts, easy to grow and rich in vitamins and proteins, take only three to five days to raise. The basic techniques and equipment are simple. Seeds can be sprouted in almost any kind of household container, and the only space they require is a dark niche in a warm place, such as a kitchen cupboard. The best-known sprouting seeds are mung bean (the sprouts are often used in Oriental dishes), soybean, and alfalfa, but many other kinds can be used including wheat, corn, barley, mustard, clover, and radish. Most health-food stores carry seeds for sprouting. Even dried peas, beans, and lentils from the grocery or supermarket make tasty, nutritious sprouts. However, you should never eat sprouts from seeds that have been sold for planting in the garden, especially if they are not certified organic; they are generally treated with a poisonous chemical fungicide. Also avoid tomato and potato sprouts, both of which are poisonous. In addition, the seed sprouts of many ornamental flowers, foliage plants, and wild plants are poisonous.

The first step in sprouting is to measure out the seeds. With most seeds ¼ cup will yield 1 to 2 cups of sprouts—enough for four average servings. Rinse the seeds thoroughly in a sieve or strainer, then soak them overnight in cool water. Allow at least four times as much water as seeds, since the seeds will absorb a great deal of moisture. The following morning, drain the seeds and place them in a clean, sterile sprouting container, such as a bowl, wide-mouthed jar, or flowerpot. Keep the seeds damp—not wet—and allow air to reach them. A shallow layer of seeds in a wide container is better than a deep layer in a narrow container. Very small seeds, such as alfalfa and clover, are more easily sprouted on a moist paper towel than in a jar. Place the towel in a shallow bowl or dish, sprinkle the presoaked seeds onto it, and cover lightly with another paper towel. Sprinkle water over the towels from time to time to keep the seeds moist. For added flavor, give alfalfa and clover sprouts a few hours of light on the last day of sprouting. Seeds should be rinsed in a strainer twice daily in cold water when they are sprouting. Discard any that are not sprouting properly, drain the rest, and return them to the container. The seed hulls should come off and float away during the last few rinses. Chickpeas and soybeans should be rinsed four to six times a day.

Most seeds sprout well at room temperature (60°F to 80°F); soybeans and chickpeas do best at about 50°F. For use in salads or juice, most sprouts should be 1 to 1 ½ in. long. Peas and lentil sprouts should be the length of the seed. As a general rule, the bigger the seed, the shorter the sprout should be for maximum flavor and tenderness. Sprouts are best when eaten fresh but will keep four to six days in the refrigerator.

Wheatgrass

According to some studies, wheatgrass increases red blood cell count and lowers blood pressure; cleanses the organs and gastrointestinal tract of debris; stimulates metabolism; fights tumors; neutralizes toxins; and restores alkalinity to the blood. Buy wheatgrass seeds (also called hard winter wheat seed or wheat berries) that are organic so that you're sure they haven't been treated with pesticides. For a 16" x 16" tray, you'll want about 2 cups of seeds. Place the seeds in a bowl, add cold, filtered water to the bowl (you'll want about 3 times as much water as you have seeds), cover the bowl, and allow to sit overnight. Drain the water from the seeds, add more water, and allow to soak for another 10 or so hours. You can also do this in a plastic container with a lid—poke tiny holes in the lid so that you can simply turn it upside down to drain the water. Repeat one more time (three soaks in all) and you should see little "tails" appearing—that means the seeds have begun to sprout. Fill your planting tray ⅔ full with organic potting soil. Sprinkle the seeds evenly over the soil and press down gently. Water the seeds until water begins to drip out the bottom of your container, and then cover the tray with a damp cloth to keep them moist. Mist the soil and the cloth twice a day for about four days, and then remove the cloth. Place your tray in spot that gets some light but isn't in direct sunlight. In about 9 to 10 days, the grass should be about 6" tall. Each blade of grass will "split," shooting out a second blade. That means it's ready to harvest. Use scissors to cut the grass just above the root. Use immediately, or keep in the refrigerator for up to a week. Keep watering the tray for a second batch of grass. You'll probably want to have two or three trays of grass growing on a rotating basis to keep a steady harvest.

Wheatgrass tends to clog some juicers, so you may want to invest in a special wheatgrass juicer. Or you can use a regular blender and then strain off the solids before adding the wheatgrass juice to your drinks.

Planting and Harvesting Guide

Basil. Start basil indoors in individual pots about 6 weeks before the last spring frost. Basil likes warm air, so heat lamps may be helpful. Choose an outdoor site that gets 6–8 hours of full sun every day. Soil should be moist and well-drained. Plant seedlings in the ground about ¼ in., deep, spaced 10–12 in. apart. Water regularly. Pick the leaves often to encourage growth, and pinch off flower heads when they appear. Harvest before the first frost. If pruned regularly, 12 basil plants will produce 4–6 cups of leaves per week. You may wish to grow some plants in pots outdoors during the summer and bring them into a sunny spot in your home during the winter months.

Beets. An easy-to-grow, dual purpose crop: both roots and greens (leaves) can be eaten or juiced. Beets are quite frost-hardy and can be planted in spring as soon as the soil is ready to work. They do well in most types of soil, except those that are highly acidic. Plant ½ in. deep, 1 in. apart in rows 18 in. apart. Thin to 2–3 in. apart. For a fall crop, plant in late June or early July. Harvest when roots are 1–3 in. in diameter (pull up one or two to check). Beets that grow larger become tough and woody. Days to harvest: 50–70. The vitamin-rich greens can also be juiced. In the warmer parts of the nation, beets are often sown in early fall for a winter crop.

Broccoli. A member of the cabbage group raised for its flower buds, which are eaten before they open. (Broccoli is not edible after it goes to seed.) Broccoli prefers cool weather and can stand light frost. It will not bear in hot weather. In very mild areas it can be grown in winter. Start broccoli indoors about six weeks before the average date of the last spring frost; set out in garden two weeks before the last expected frost date. Space plants 15–18 in. apart in rows 2 ½–3 ft. apart. Harvest while flower buds are tight and heads compact. Cut off about 6 in. below the head so as not to waste the tender, edible upper stem. After the center heads (the first to develop) are cut, side shoots will develop additional heads. One plant yields six to eight cuttings over a period of 8–10 weeks. Days to harvest: 55–60, 75 for fall crops. For a fall harvest sow directly in the garden around midsummer. Broccoli retains its flavor and texture well when frozen, and it is an excellent source of Vitamins A and C.

Cabbage. A cool-weather crop that can be raised for spring or fall harvest. Cabbage is a good source of Vitamin C and keeps well in winter. Types include the familiar green cabbage, the mild-flavored, crinkly-leafed savoy, and the colorful red cabbage. A heavy feeder, cabbage needs a rich, nearly neutral soil that contains plenty of organic matter. For spring cabbage start seeds indoors about six to eight weeks before the last expected frost. Transplant to the garden after danger of frost is past—cabbage seedlings exposed to frost or cold grow slowly and tend to be fibrous and tough. Plants should be spaced 12–18 in. apart in rows 2–3 ft. apart. For fall crops start seeds indoors in May and set out after midsummer, or sow directly in the garden June to August—the milder the winter, the later you should sow. For direct sowing, plant seeds in groups of three or four, ½ in. deep at 1-ft. intervals in the rows; thin later to the one strongest seedling. Cabbage thrives with an insulating mulch of hay or straw to keep the soil cool. Harvest cabbage when the heads are tight and full. Days to harvest: 50–90. Fall cabbage develops larger heads and—many people think—better flavor than spring cabbage. Several soil-borne diseases attack cabbage and its close relatives, such as broccoli, cauliflower, and turnips. To avoid infection, do not plant any member of the cabbage family in soil where any of them has been grown in the last two years.

Cantaloupe. An orange-fleshed melon with a netted exterior. Cantaloupe (a kind of muskmelon) needs a long, warm growing season and full exposure to the sun. Early-maturing dwarf varieties are recommended for northern gardens. Since cold is bad for melons (cool temperatures and rain lower the quantity of sugar), they should not be planted until dependably warm weather, several weeks after the last frost. Like other melons, cantaloupes do best in sandy soil with plenty of manure and compost mixed in. To plant in rows, sow seeds ½ in. deep, 4–6 in. apart in rows 5 ft. apart and thin to 18–24 in. apart. Alternatively, plant three to a hill, with the hills 5 ft. apart each way. Figure on about four fruits per plant. In colder regions start the melons indoors three to four weeks ahead of planting time. Melons need ample water while the fruits are growing, but during the final ripening stage limiting the water is said to increase their sweetness. Cantaloupes are ready to pick when the fruit separates from the stem with a slight pull. Days to harvest: 60–90. If any fruits form after midsummer, pick them off the vine; they will not ripen and will take food from the others.

Carrots. One of the old standbys, high in Vitamin A and excellent for juicing. Carrots are a hardy vegetable that can be planted in spring as soon as the soil can be worked. Since the seeds are slow to germinate, it is helpful to plant radish seeds along with them to mark the row. The radishes will be ready to harvest about the time the carrots start coming up. Carrots do best in rich, deep, sandy loam but will grow well in almost any soil that has been properly prepared. Dig up the soil to a depth of at least 1 ft., loosen it, and remove stones and other debris. This will allow the downward-growing carrot roots to develop properly. Heavy clay soils often cause carrots to fork. Lighten such soils by working in a goodly proportion of sand or humus. Sow carrot seeds ¼–½ in. deep, 15 to 20 seeds to the inch in rows 16–24 in. apart. Thin the seedlings to 2 in. apart when they are 2–4 in. high, or when the roots are about as thick as your little finger (pull up a few carrots to check root size). The tender baby carrots that have been thinned out make delicious eating. The remaining carrots may be harvested at any time, depending on how large you want them. Keep the soil moist until the seedlings have come up. For a fall crop, sow in the garden in early July. Carrots keep well in the refrigerator or in winter storage.

Cauliflower. A "luxury" member of the cabbage group that is difficult for beginners to grow successfully. Cauliflower needs rich soil and constant moisture for best development. It is sensitive to heat, requiring a long, cool growing season to produce good heads. Cauliflower does best as a fall crop in most areas. For a fall crop, seeds may be sown directly in the garden in June or July, 8–10 weeks before the first expected autumn frost date for your locality. Plant seeds three or four together, ½ in. deep and 18–24 in. apart and thin to the strongest single seedling. For a spring crop start indoors in February or March and set out a week before the last average frost date. Plants should be no older than six weeks when set out. Set seedlings 18 in. apart in rows 30 in. apart. When heads are about 3 in. across, they should be blanched—that is, the leaves should be tied over them (this will produce white heads). Harvest while heads are compact and fairly smooth (two to four weeks after tying up, depending on the weather). Days to harvest: 50–95, depending on variety.

Celery. One of the trickier plants for the home gardener to raise. Celery is very sensitive to both cold and heat and requires a growing season of four months. Consequently, it must be started indoors in March or April and set out in the garden between June 15 and July 15. Plants should be 6 in. apart in rows 18–24 in. apart. Celery needs a constantly moist soil very rich in organic matter; muck soils are the best. For maximum growth celery should be fertilized every two weeks. Celery stalks are naturally green but can be blanched (whitened) by various means. You can hill up dirt around the plants, place boards along the sides of the rows, or cover the plants with drain tiles, paper, or mulch. Blanching is not recommended for the home garden because of the extra space required and the danger of rot. Days to harvest: 115–135. Note: Celery may be harvested before fully mature. While celery is primarily raised for its crunchy stalks, the nutty root, or "heart," is a delicacy. The leaves are used for flavoring soups and stews.

Collards. A loose-leafed relative of the cabbage. A traditional southern favorite, collards thrive in almost every section of the country. They are an excellent source of Vitamin A. Collards tolerate cold as low as 15°F, and frost actually improves their flavor. They also tolerate hot summers better than cabbage and will grow in relatively poor soil. In areas with short, cool summers, sow collards in late spring. Elsewhere, sow them in midsummer for a fall crop. Plant seeds ½ in. deep and 1 in. apart in rows 24–30 in. apart. Thin so plants are 18–24 in. apart along the rows; the thinnings can be used as greens. Harvest by clipping the young leaves, including the stems. Be sure to leave six to eight leaves on the plant: they are needed to sustain growth. Do not harvest the central growing point or you will have to wait for side shoots to form to provide new leaves. Days to harvest: 75–80. In the Deep South collards are grown through the winter to furnish fresh greens.

Cucumbers. Not the easiest vegetable to grow but a good yielder with a long harvesting season. Sow outdoors when soil is warm and danger of frost is past. Plant seeds ½–1 in. deep, 4–6 in. apart in rows 5 ft. apart; thin 12–15 in. to give the vines room to grow. Cucumbers can also be planted in hills 5 ft. apart each way, 5 to 10 seeds per hill; thin later to three to four plants per hill. For a head start plant seeds indoors four to eight weeks before the last frost date. Cucumbers need ample moisture and do best in a deep, rich, neutral soil. Well-rotted manure mixed into the soil is helpful. Plants should be watered throughout the growing season: insufficient water results in undersized, misshapen fruits. Mulching helps retain soil moisture and protects fruits by keeping them off the soil. Cucumber vines are eager climbers and may be trained on poles, fences, frameworks, or wire netting. These methods of saving space are preferable for the small garden. Some cucumbers are bred for pickling, others for salad use—salad cucumbers are best for juicing. Pick salad cucumbers when 6–9 in. long. Cucumbers must be picked before they turn yellow—at this stage the seeds harden and the fruit loses flavor. Keeping the vines picked stimulates them to produce until frost kills them; the presence of big, ripe cukes on the vines halts fruit production. Days to harvest: 50–70, depending on variety. Each cucumber vine bears separate male and female flowers (except for certain all-female hybrids). No fruits are produced until the female flowers appear (identifiable by a tiny cucumber beneath the blossom). Since the vines grow from the tip only, do not break their tips off, as this will stop their growth. To avoid spreading disease, do not handle the vines or harvest the fruits when they are wet. Despite old wives' tales to the contrary, cucumbers do not cross with squash and melons.

Garlic. Garlic should be planted in the fall in a sunny spot with well-drained, rich, loamy soil. To prepare the cloves for planting, fill a jar with water, a tablespoon of baking soda, and a tablespoon of liquid seaweed, and soak them for about 3 hours. This will help protect them from fungal diseases. Plant each clove with the pointed tip facing up. The tip should be about 2 in. below the soil surface. Top with mulch. In the spring, make sure the garlic bed stays moist. In early summer, you should see curly sprouts coming out of the ground. These mature into long, thin stalks that should be trimmed and can be used in cooking. In late June or early July, you'll notice the leaves tuning yellowish-brown. When they're about half turned, dig up the bulbs, tie together the stalks, and hang in a shady, dry place for 4–6 weeks. They can then be stored in a cool, dry place for several months.

Ginger. Buy a piece of organic ginger root. Look for one that is plump and firm. Soak it overnight in warm water. Buds should begin to form. You can plant ginger in a pot or, if you live in a tropical climate, in the ground. Plant the ginger in a shady spot 1–2 in. beneath the soil, with the eye buds pointing up. Plant each root about 12 in. apart. If there are several eye buds on your root, you can divide it into a few pieces and plant each. Water lightly. The soil should stay fairly dry until the shoots begin to appear, then water more heavily. In about a year, your ginger plant should be 2–4 ft. tall. You can dig up the roots to use after about 8 months, but the longer you wait, the bigger the root will get.

Kale. A good source of Vitamin C and thiamin. Kale can tolerate summer heat and is extremely cold-hardy. It can be raised as a spring or fall crop. Sow in spring as soon as soil can be worked, ¼ in. deep, 1 in. apart in rows 20 in. apart; thin to 12 in. between plants. About 5 ft. of row per person should furnish an adequate supply. For fall and early winter harvesting, sow in midsummer. Harvest by taking entire plant or by cutting the outer leaves only, leaving the inner ones to develop. Days to harvest: 60–70, depending on variety. Kale can be covered with straw or burlap and kept fresh and green in the garden until very cold weather. South of Virginia, this protection is usually not necessary.

Lettuce. A cool-weather crop available in either head or looseleaf types and in many varieties of each. All varieties will provide a bountiful harvest of salad greens until summer heat stimulates the plants to flower, which makes them tough and bitter. Lettuce can also be sown in late summer for a fall crop. Lettuce is one of the easiest vegetables to raise from seed. Sow thinly in early spring, ¼ in. deep in rows 16 in. apart. Thin gradually to 12 in. between plants for loose-leaf types, 16–18 in. for head types. (Head lettuce is often started indoors in flats and set out when the soil is ready to work.) Thin ruthlessly—lettuce needs a lot of room to grow in. Thinnings may be transplanted or used thriftily in a garden-fresh salad. To be tender and free from bitterness, lettuce should grow quickly. It needs plenty of water and nitrogen. To keep leaf lettuce producing for a maximum length of time, harvest only the outer leaves so that the plant continuously produces new leaves for use. With head lettuce the entire head must be harvested. Head lettuce is more sensitive to heat than loose-leaf lettuce. The growing season for both types can often be prolonged by planting them in a partly shaded area of the garden. Days to harvest: 40–83. For a fall crop sow in August. Lettuce seeds will not sprout when the soil temperature is more than 80°F, but they can be forced to germinate by chilling them in the refrigerator in damp peat moss and sand for five days.

Mint. Mint plants are perennials and tend to spread like crazy. Most varieties are hardy in Zones 3–8. Choose a cool spot in partial shade and be sure the soil is moist and loamy. It's easiest to start with a potted mint plant or cuttings from a friend's plant. Keep them potted, or transplant to the garden. Harvest the leaves as desired.

Peppers. A frost-tender crop that needs a long, warm growing season. In their tropical home pepper plants are perennials and reach the size of small trees. In the mainland United States they are raised as annuals and grow about 2 ft. tall. There are sweet and hot types of peppers. All varieties have much the same cultural requirements as tomatoes, to which they are related. They do best on a slightly acidic soil with full sun and plenty of moisture. For most areas of the United States peppers should be started indoors about eight weeks before the last expected frost date and set out in the garden when the soil is warm. The plants should be 18–24 in. apart in rows 24–36 in. apart. Three to five plants per person are sufficient. The fruits of both sweet and hot peppers may be harvested at any stage of growth. Sweet peppers, also known as green or bell peppers, turn red or yellow at maturity. At this stage they are sweeter. Some hot peppers turn red or yellow soon after the fruits are formed. Be careful when picking peppers: the plants are brittle, and you may end up with a whole branch in your hand instead of a fruit. You can avoid the problem by cutting the fruits off, not picking them. Peppers are temperamental plants. They set fruit only when nighttime temperatures are between 60° and 70°F. If they do not get enough moisture, they drop blossoms and fruits. However, under favorable conditions they bear plentifully. Sweet peppers are rich in Vitamin C and freeze well; hot peppers can be stored by stringing them up and letting them dry. In fall, sweet peppers can be kept for two to three weeks by pulling up the entire plant and hanging it, roots uppermost, in a cool (but not freezing) indoor location. Pepper plants can be grown indoors in pots in wintertime or where garden space is limited.

Pumpkin. A kind of squash first cultivated by American Indians. Whether they are the vine or bush type, pumpkins require a great deal of space; however, in a small garden they can be grown on a trellis with the fruits supported by slings. Pumpkins grow 7–24 in. in diameter, depending on type. In general, the smaller varieties are better for eating. Large pumpkins were used for stock feed on the old-time family farm. There are also special varieties that are raised for their tasty seeds. Frost-tender, as are all members of the gourd family, pumpkins should not be planted until all danger of frost is past and the soil is warm. They may be started indoors three to four weeks before the last expected frost date. For outdoor planting, plant seeds in hills 8–10 ft. apart for vine types, 4–6 ft. for bush types. Plant six seeds to the hill; when seedlings are about 6 in. tall, thin out all but the two or three strongest ones. A shovelful of manure or compost mixed in with the soil will get the plants off to a good start. For pumpkins started indoors use two or three to a hill. Pumpkins may also be planted in rows, with 3–4 ft. of space between plants and at least 6 ft. between rows to allow room for the sprawling vines. Mulching is recommended to keep down weeds, conserve soil moisture, and keep the fruits off the dirt. On the old-time farm pumpkins were often planted with corn, a practice settlers had learned from the Indians. To grow huge exhibition-type pumpkins, plant seeds of a large variety such as Big Max or Mammoth. Allow only one fruit to develop on each vine and water the plants heavily. Pumpkins are normally left on the vine until the vine is killed by frost or deteriorates from age. (The fruits, with their thick skins, are not harmed by a light frost.) The best practice is to cut the stem a few inches above the fruit. Store pumpkins in a cool, dry place. Days to harvest: 100–120 for most varieties.

Spinach. A hardy cool-weather vegetable that yields both spring and fall crops. Spinach is rich in Vitamin A and a good source of iron. Most spinach contains small amounts of oxalic acid, an agent that causes loss of calcium from the blood. New strains are available; however, they have almost none of this substance. Spinach thrives on well-drained, fertile soils with plenty of organic matter. The soil should be slightly acid; on very acid or very alkaline soils spinach does poorly. Plant seeds four to six weeks before the last expected frost date, ½ in. deep and about 1 in. apart in rows 14 in. apart. Thin to 4 in. between plants. Harvest spinach by picking the outer leaves as soon as they reach edible size. Should buds form at the center, it is a sign that the plant will soon bolt (send up its flower stalk) and its leaves will become tough and unpalatable. At the bud stage the plants are still good and can be salvaged by pulling them up or cutting them off at ground level. Long days and hot weather in combination stimulate spinach to bolt. For a fall crop, plant in late August or early September. Because of its short growing life, spinach should be planted in small batches at two-week intervals. Spinach can be grown as a winter vegetable in areas where temperatures do not dip much below the freezing point. Days to harvest: 40–50.

Strawberries. Purchase young strawberry plants to plant in the spring after the last frost. Try to find plants that are certified disease-free, since diseases from strawberries can spread through your whole garden. Strawberries thrive with lots of sun and well-drained soil. If you have access to a gentle south-facing slope, this is ideal. Till the top 12 in. of soil. If you planted a cover crop, turn under all the organic matter. If not, be sure to add manure or compost to a reach a rich, slightly acidic soil. Dig a 5- to 7-in. wide hole for each plant. It should be deep enough to accommodate the root system without squishing it. Place the plant in the hole and fill in the soil, tamping it down gently around the plant. Space plants about 12 in. apart on all sides. The roots will shoot out runners that produce more small plants. To allow the plants to focus their energy on fruit production, snip the runners and transplant or discard any new plants. An alternate planting method is the matted-row system. This method requires less maintenance but offers a slightly lower quality yield. Space plants about 18 in. apart, allowing the roots to shoot out runners and produce new plants. If planting more than one row, space them three to four feet apart. To aid picking and to keep the plants from competing with each other, prune out the plants on the outer edges of rows by snipping the runners and pulling out the plants.

Tomatoes. Tomatoes are among the best yielders of all vegetables but need a long growing season with moderate temperatures—they will not set fruit when nighttime temperatures are below 60°F or above 75°F, to many a gardener's puzzlement and dismay. Years of experimentation, research, and controlled breeding have resulted in a profusion of special varieties. Tomatoes are available that range in size from giant 1-lb. Big Boy hybrids down to tiny plum and cherry tomatoes. There are egg-shaped and pear-shaped tomatoes. In addition to the familiar red, there are orange, yellow, and pink tomatoes (orange and yellow types tend to be sweeter, with less bite). There are bushy dwarf strains that can be grown in a pot or window box. Early, midseason, and late-ripening varieties have also been developed. Most early types are so-called determinate tomatoes—the vines grow to a certain length, bear their fruit over a short period, and then die. Midseason and late-season varieties are usually indeterminate—the vines continue to grow and bear fruit until the onset of cold weather stops them. Since tomatoes are killed by frost and grow poorly at cooler temperatures, they are usually started indoors in all but the warmest parts of the country. Start the seeds six to eight weeks before the last expected frost date, and set out when the weather is safely warm. To save time and trouble, you can buy ready-to-plant seedlings at most garden-supply centers and supermarkets and at many neighborhood stores as well. However, only the top-selling varieties tend to be available. Tomatoes do best in slightly acidic soil and need plenty of water. Before setting out the seedlings, dig compost, well-rotted manure, or damp peat moss into the soil to improve its moisture-holding capacity. Place the plants 2–3 ft. apart in rows 3 ft. apart. The vines may either be allowed to sprawl on the ground, which gives a higher yield, or trained on stakes, fences, or other supports. A popular method is to train the vines on a circular "tower" of heavy wire. The advantage of training is that the vines yield cleaner fruit and are easier to inspect and pick. Mulching is helpful, especially if the vines have been left to grow on the ground. Tomatoes that are trained above the ground should be pruned to one or two main stems. This is done by pinching or cutting off the suckers next to the main stems. (Suckers are shoots that grow in the joints where the leaf stems meet the main stem; if allowed to grow, they divert energy from fruit production.) Suckers should be pinched off throughout the growing season. However, do not remove foliage to let sunlight reach the fruits. Instead of aiding them to ripen, it causes sun scald, a discoloration and toughening of the skin. Tomatoes are ripe when they separate easily from the stem. If cool or rainy weather delays ripening, they may be picked as soon as they start to change color and ripened on a sunny windowsill. To pick unripe tomatoes, twist them off the vine. Tomatoes can be stored for several weeks in fall by pulling up the entire plant and hanging it upside down in a cool, shady place. The tomatoes will ripen slowly on the vine. Unripe tomatoes may also be picked and stored in a single layer. Rich in Vitamins A and C, tomatoes are excellent for canning and freezing. Days to harvest: 52–90, depending on variety.

Watermelon. One of the gourd family raised for its sweet, juicy fruit. Watermelons need a warm growing season, plentiful moisture, and full sun for proper growth and flavor (even a light frost can kill them). Standard melons reach sizes of 20 lb. and up and are best grown in the warmer sections of the country. For cooler regions, midget varieties are available. They weigh 4–15 lb. and mature in a shorter time. In all but the warmest areas watermelons should be started indoors about four weeks before the last expected frost date and set out when the nights are reliably warm (above 55°F). Watermelons are usually planted in hills, at least 6 ft. apart in each direction, two seedlings to a hill. If planted in rows, the plants should be 2–3 ft. apart in rows 6–7 ft. apart. Mulch is very helpful in preventing the fruit from rotting. There is no sure way of telling when a watermelon is ready to harvest. One traditional method is to thump the melon; a hollow sound indicates it is ripe. Another is to examine the underside of the melon. When it turns yellow, the melon is probably ripe. Days to harvest: 70–95, depending on variety.

Recipe Index

METRIC AND IMPERIAL CONVERSIONS
(These conversions are rounded for convenience)

Ingredient	Cups/Tablespoons/ Teaspoons	Ounces	Grams/Milliliters
Flour, all-purpose	1 cup/1 tablespoon	4.5 ounces/0.3 ounce	125 grams/8 grams
Flour, whole wheat	1 cup	4 ounces	120 grams
Fruits or veggies, chopped	1 cup	5 to 7 ounces	145 to 200 grams
Honey, maple syrup, or corn syrup	1 tablespoon	.75 ounce	20 grams
Liquids: cream, milk, water, or juice	1 cup	8 fluid ounces	240 milliliters
Oats	1 cup	5.5 ounces	150 grams
Salt	1 teaspoon	0.2 ounces	6 grams
Spices: cinnamon, cloves, ginger, or nutmeg (ground)	1 teaspoon	0.2 ounce	5 milliliters
Sugar, brown, firmly packed	1 cup	7 ounces	200 grams
Sugar, white	1 cup/1 tablespoon	7 ounces/0.5 ounce	200 grams/12.5 grams
Vanilla extract	1 teaspoon	0.2 ounce	4 grams